Robert W. James

# Python Programming for Absolute Beginners

*A simple and practical guide for people with zero programming knowledge*

# Introduction

So, you want to learn how to code and write programs? If you do, then maybe this book is just what you need. But why use Python? It's a rather strange sounding programming language and if you look at the blue and yellow icons used for this language, you would think that it is something funky.

But there are advantages inherent in the Python programming language that makes it a pretty good choice for absolute newbies to learn how to code. It also introduces the newcomer to a lot of programming concepts without the usual constraints of strict syntax and the other restrictive rules of other programming languages.

Python is no less than one of the most popular programming languages today. As far as other programming languages go, this one is classified as a high-level programming language.

That means the words and terms used in Python closely resemble modern-day English. That means you don't need to learn a lot of jargon.

It also has plenty of real life applications such as artificial intelligence, scientific computing, scripting, and web programming. That's a lot of applications that you can aim for in the future as you learn more about programming in general.

But let's not get ahead of ourselves.

You will not be creating AI after reading this book. You won't be able to create an app that can do big data analytics after learning the fundamental programming concepts in this book.

*Let's keep our expectations realistic.*

It is assumed that the reader of this book has no prior knowledge of programming whatsoever. In short, you don't come from a programming related background.

That means everything that you will learn here in these pages are the absolute basics.

The goal of this book is to teach you the fundamental principles of writing a computer program using Python. You will learn how to formulate logical instructions that a computer can follow. You will also learn how programs flow from one line to the next, and so on.

Along the way, you will learn the ins and outs of the Python programming language from how to download it for free all the way to running Python programs that provide solutions to a variety of potential real-life problems.

This book will contain a few quizzes and some programming exercises that you can try. They are designed to help you gauge how much you have learned and put to practice the concepts that you have internalized. These exercises also help you think outside the box.

Not all the answers are provided here but if you review the discussion within that chapter, it will help you find the answers there.

Remember, this book is designed to be a complete beginner's guide. If you already have intermediate experience in programming then this book is not for you.

Now, if you're ready to jump right in, head on over to chapter 1 where you will get a short introduction to the Python programming language, its history, how to install it, and how to run it on your computer to get you started writing your very first lines of programming code.

Once again, thanks for purchasing this book, I hope you find it to be helpful!

# Table of Contents

# Chapter 1: Setting Things Up

Before you can start programming in Python, the first thing you need to do is to set up your tools. This means finding the appropriate software and installing them on your computer.

Remember that the Python programming language is designed to run across different platforms. What that means is that you can run Python on different operating systems like Windows, Mac, Linux, and others.

Note that if you are running Mac or Linux on your computer, it will have Python pre-installed on your system. If it is, what you need to do is to update your version of Python—that means you still need to download it anyway.

Another thing that you need to know is that it is open-source software. That simply means it is free to download, install, and use. It also means anyone can modify this programming language as needed.

## How to Download and Install Python: The Usual Way

To download and install the latest version of Python, you need to go to the official Python website, which you will find by clicking here. Choose the version for your computer's operating system.

After downloading the installer, run the file and follow the prompts during the installation. You may choose certain options like the installation path and running Python from anywhere on your computer, among others.

When you install Python from their official website, the installation will come with an IDE, which is short for an integrated development environment.

**Side Note – What is an IDE?** An IDE is a software program or app that includes different tools that you will use to build a computer program. It comes with a text editor that allows you to type programming code, tools to test your program (also known as a debugger), and tools that allow you to build code automatically. Think of it as a kind of all-in-one software that you can use to write, edit, and complete computer programs.

Some IDEs can be used to write code for different programming languages. The IDE that comes with your Python installation is called IDLE. This one is specifically designed only for working on Python code.

## Python's Immediate Mode

After you have installed Python on your computer, you can run in directly by typing "python" on the command line.

You can pin that to the taskbar or start menu, if you're using Windows. When you run that, you will see a black command screen, which will look something like this:

```
Microsoft Windows [Version 10.0.17134.648]
(c) 2018 Microsoft Corporation. All rights reserved.

C:\Users\ASUS>python
Python 3.7.2 (tags/v3.7.2:9a3ffc0492, Dec 23 2018, 22:20:52
) [MSC v.1916 32 bit (Intel)] on win32
Type "help", "copyright", "credits" or "license" for more i
nformation.
>>> 1 + 1
2
>>> quit()

C:\Users\ASUS>_
```

This black screen is the Immediate Mode in Python. You can directly type Python programming lines at the >>> prompt. For example, type "5 + 5" on that prompt (don't include the double quotes).

Hit enter after typing a line of math. See if it displays the sum of that mathematical expression. You will use Immediate Mode for instant code running and testing. If you think you forgot how a certain line in Python goes or if you want to see if a certain piece of syntax will work, then you can try it here in Immediate Mode.

## Python's Included IDE

When you type programming code, the lines or instructions that you type will be saved in a Python script file. It will be something like a document that you type in MS Word or any text editor. The difference is that it will contain Python code and the file will not have a .docx extension but a .py extension.

You will type and save your code in the integrated development environment. Again, the IDE included in your Python installation is called IDLE.

To run IDLE, you will follow the same steps as before. Type the word "IDLE" (minus the double quotes) on the command prompt, just like you did for Immediate Mode. After you hit enter, you will see something like the following screen:

## An Easier Way to Install Python

If all of that sounds too complicated for you, then there are other ways to have Python installed on your computer. The alternative is actually the easier way to do it. This programming language is included when you install certain integrated development environments, like Thonny IDE for instance.

If you want to try and download Thonny on your computer, you can download the IDE here.

Installing it is pretty easy. Installing other IDEs that come with Python is pretty much the same way.

1. Download the installer file from the official website (link for Thonny provided above).
2. Run the installer after the download has completed
3. Follow the prompts on the installation wizard
4. You can also customize the installation by selecting which folders to use and which files to associate with the system

## Installing Python on Your Phone or Mobile Device

You can't technically "install" Python on your phone. But it can run on your phone through an app. Let's go over how to install Pydroid – the app that has Python for Android.

1. Open the Play Store
2. Search for Pydroid – the latest version as of this writing is Pydroid 3. It's only 48 megabytes so downloading it will be really quick.
3. After the app is downloaded and installed you can run it right away.

Note that you don't need to be online to write and run your code on Pydroid. You can type the code on your screen and it will look something like this:

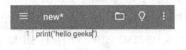

To run the commands/code that you typed, just click the yellow button at the bottom right.

Now that you have Python installed, we can start writing some simple codes that you can test. In the next chapter, we'll go over some exercises to help you get started in writing code in this programming language.

# Key Takeaways:

- Python is free to download and install
- It is a multipurpose language
- It can be installed on your computer and mobile device
- You can install it with an IDE, or just install it directly from the official source site and it also comes with its own native IDE
- You will use IDEs to type and run code using Python

# Chapter 2: Input and Output

Now that you have Python installed on your device, one of the first things that you can do to have some fun with this programming language is to display something on the screen and then ask for user input.

These are input and output operations in programming. Output means using data or information generated via your programming code and then transmitting that to an actual device or component such as the screen, a printer, a projector, or speakers.

In this initial exercise, we will output text to the screen. The text can be read by the users of your computer program. We will cover input later in this chapter.

## Displaying Output in Python

To display output in this programming language, you will need to use something called a function—specifically the print( ) function (yes, it has an open and close parenthesis with it).

**What is a Function?** In Python programming, a function is actually a bunch of commands that have been grouped together into a single statement. In the case of the print( ) function, it automatically gathers data that will be outputted

and then displays the data as it were to the device's screen—
if it's a computer then the data is displayed on the monitor

But if you're using your phone then the output will be
displayed on your phone's screen. Note that the screen (any
screen where a program is running) is often designated as
the standard output device.

The print( ) function is only one of many functions in this
programming language. Later on, as you learn more about Python
you will also learn how to make your own functions as well.

## Using the Print( ) Function for Basic Output

To start coding, you should first launch Python's immediate mode.
If you need help with that, please review chapter 1.

Once you have the blinking cursor in immediate mode's black
screen, you should type the following exactly as it is:

```
print('This sentence will be displayed on the screen')
```

After typing that line on the black screen, press Enter. You will then
see the text inside the quotation marks displayed in the next line.

It should look something like this:

Notice that the command or programming code is the one on the line that has the ">>>" and the output is in the line after it. Only the text that is inside the quotation marks will be displayed on the

```
Python 3.7 (32-bit)
Python 3.7.4 (tags/v3.7.4:e09359112e, Jul  8 2019, 19:29:22) [MSC v.1916 32 bit (Intel)] on win32
Type "help", "copyright", "credits" or "license" for more information.
>>> print('This sentence will be displayed on the screen')
This sentence will be displayed on the screen
>>>
```

screen.


Programming Exercises


1. Use the print( ) function to display your name on the screen.
2. This time display numbers instead of letters.
3. After that output a combination of numbers and letters, let's say your birth date.


The programming above will help you get comfy with using Python's immediate mode. Remember that you will use it to try out different commands and programming code. A more efficient way to write programming code is by using an integrated development environment or IDE, which was mentioned earlier. We'll look into how you can use an IDE later on in this book.

## Displaying Text in the Next Line

Sometimes you want the output to be displayed on several lines. With the exercises that you have done, all of the text is on a single line. What if you want to display it on several lines?

So, here's a question, how do you display text like this:

```
1
2
3
```

What commands or commands will you use? Some would say you

```
>>> print('1')
1
>>> print('2')
2
>>> print('3')
3
>>>
```

should use multiple print( ) functions to display each number in a different line. That will work when you use an IDE to write the code in Python. But you can't do it in immediate mode since you will have several prompts in between, which would look like this:

## Control Structures

Here's the solution. Python and other programming languages have control structures that change the behavior of functions and programming statements. In this case, the control structures are called *arguments*—and that's not a line from Monty Python. I'm not trying to have an argument with you (grin!).

The print( ) function actually has several arguments. But we will introduce you first to the '\n' argument. When you add this argument to any text that you want to display, it will display the other text after it on the next line.

To demonstrate that, try the following line of code on Python's immediate mode:

```
print('This is the first line\nand this is the second')
```

Enter that line of code on your screen and then hit enter. You will notice that everything before the '\n' will be printed on the first line on top and then those that come after it are displayed on the next line.

Programming Exercise

1. Use the print( ) function to display the numbers 1, 2, and 3 on three different lines.

Review Questions

1. What is a function in Python programming?
2. What type of programming object is the "\n" control structure?

3. What practical uses/applications would the print( ) function have other than just displaying characters on the screen?

# input() Function for User Input in Python

To make your Python programs more interactive, you can add input statements to them. An input statement is a programming structure that receives data that is supplied by the user.

**What is a Programming Statement?** A programming statement, or simply a statement, is a line of code in any programming language that gives the computer an exact action that needs to be taken or performed.

A great real-world example of its use in tandem with the print( ) function is asking for the user's password. You can use the print( ) statement to make a short explanation about what the user is to enter. And then you will use another statement/function to prompt the user to enter his or her password and take the data entered by the user.

To allow users to enter data using their keyboards, you will use the input( ) function in Python programming.

Here's an example of how you can use the input( ) function. Try the following line of code in immediate mode:

```
>>> serialnumber = input('Enter your serial number: ')
```

The difference here is that the input( ) function is on the right side of the operator above whereas the print( ) function is on the left and is the first word in your line of code. We have a new term or word in that line of code up there, it's this one:

serialnumber

Note that this is a user supplied word. What that means is that it is a word that you, the programmer, create within the code. There are reserved words in Python that have special meaning such as "input" and "print" and you can't use them for any other purpose other than what they were designed for.

We'll go over the reserved words and user supplied words in the next chapter.

**BIG TIP:** each statement or function has its own syntax or rules on how to write computer code. Remember that each programming language has its own rules on syntax.

The good news is that the syntax in Python is way easier compared to the strict syntactical rules in programming languages like C or Pascal or Visual Basic and others.

As we go through every function and statement here in Python we will also cover how the syntax works.

So, what happens if you made a mistake on the syntax of any statement? If you do your IDE or Python's immediate mode will show you an error message and it will not execute or perform the instructions in your program code.

---

# Key Takeaways:

- Input and output statements in programming make your code more interactive
- Functions are groups of organized lines of code that perform a specific action
- Arguments are control structures that change the behavior of functions and statements
- The print( ) function is used to display character strings to the screen and the input( ) function is used to accept user supplied data from the keyboard.

# Chapter 3: Making Names and Using Names

Okay, let's pick-up where we left off in the previous chapter. Remember that we didn't fully discuss the input( ) function. We need to cover a small detail or programming concept first before we can completely go over that function.

## Keywords and Identifiers in Python

We introduced you to user supplied words in Python programming in the discussion of the input( ) function. In the previous sample code, we used the following line:

>>> serialnumber = input('Enter your serial number: ')

The user-supplied term "serialnumber" is known as an identifier in Python programming. Just like anything in this language, there are syntax rules for using identifiers as well.

**What is an Identifier?** An identifier in Python is any word that is used as names for certain programming structures like objects, modules, classes, functions, and variables. Anything that is used as a name for something is

26

called an identifier. Its purpose is to identify and differentiate one programming construct from another.

## Identifier vs. Keyword

Earlier in the previous chapter we mentioned that certain words are reserved in Python—which means they already serve a specific purpose in the language, which is why you can't use them as user-defined identifiers.

Two examples of these are print and input. Both of these words or identifiers already have a purpose—i.e. they identify as it were two different functions in Python (one for input and one for output).

Don't worry. There are only a few reserved words in this programming language and you still have a lot of words to choose from. Here is a list of all the reserved words or keywords in Python:

- False
- True
- async
- assert
- as
- and
- None
- elif
- del
- def
- continue
- class
- break

- await
- if
- global
- from
- for
- finally
- except
- else
- or
- not
- nonlocal
- is
- in
- import
- yield
- with
- while
- try
- return
- raise
- pass

## Identifier Syntax

As stated earlier, there are syntax rules when you write code using identifiers. Here are the ones that you should keep in mind. A lot of beginners make mistakes regarding the syntax rules mentioned below.

1. Identifier names are case sensitive. That means when X and x are used as identifiers in your code, each one is different and unique from one another.

   Here's a little programming exercise: Assign the value 10 to the identifier X and then assign the value of 5 to the identifier x. After that, print both variables.

   To do that you should type the following lines of code in immediate mode:

   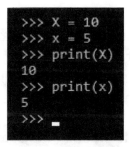

   ```
   >>> X = 10
   >>> x = 5
   >>> print(X)
   10
   >>> print(x)
   5
   >>>
   ```

2. You should use words and names that make sense and mean something to the program. So, let's say you want a portion of the program to contain the employee password. One good idea is to use the word "password" as the identifier for that value.

Here's an example:

```
>>> password = 'jeremy'

>>> print(password)

jeremy
```

Try that in immediate mode as well. Some newbie programmers become sloppy when they create identifier names. This is especially true when it comes to numbers and figures. Some would use x, y, j, and others but then you forget what purpose each one of them has within your code.

So, instead of just using X for the birth date of the user, why not just use "birthday" as your identifier? That way when your code is already around several hundred lines long, next time you see "birthday" in the code, you already know what type of data or value it holds.

3. Identifiers can be of any length. Even though Python is not particular about how long identifier names, but please don't make the code extra-long because you chose very long names.

   Best practice indicates that you should keep it short enough but still makes sense. For instance, instead of using "storemanagersalary" why not just use "mgrsalary" — the abbreviated version will still make sense when you read the code and it won't be as long.

4. You're not allowed to use special symbols when creating names. Examples of which are %, $, #, @, !

among others. The only symbol that is allowed for identifier names is an underscore.

5. You can't use keywords. Please go over the list of keywords mentioned earlier in this chapter so you can remember each one of them. As you gain more experience writing code in Python, the more familiar you will be with these keywords.

   Note that in case you forget and use one of these keywords as identifiers, Python or your IDE will give you an error message.

6. Identifier names can't begin or start with a number. So "1payment" is not allowed but "payment1" is allowed.

7. You can combine letters and numbers plus an underscore (or two) if you like to identifier names. Here are examples of allowed combinations: _payment1, payment_1, Payment1, PAY1, PAYment_1

## Using the input( ) Function

Now that we have identifiers and its related syntax rules out of the way, we can now move on to how you can use the input( ) function.

Let's go back to the example we used in chapter 2 of this book:

```
>>> serialnumber = input('Enter your serial number: ')
```

Quick Questions:

Here's a little test or learning checkpoint to see what you have learned so far. Please answer the questions below. You will find the answers in the Key Takeaways section at the end of this chapter:

1. Can you use "input" as an identifier?
2. Can you use "Serialnumber" instead of "serialnumber" as an identifier?
3. "26-serialnumber" is a valid identifier, true or false?
4. Will the identifier "serialnumber" in the example above contain letters, numbers, or a combination of alphanumeric data?

How the input( ) Function Works

Here is the official syntax used for the input( ) function:

input( prompt )

In that syntax, we know that "input" is the keyword for the function. The "prompt" is any text that will be displayed on the screen. Its purpose is to tell the user what to enter on the blinking cursor that will appear.

Note that the prompt in the input( ) function is an optional argument. You can use that function even without the prompt.

Let's go back to the example earlier:

>>> serialnumber = input('Enter your serial number: ')

In this example the text "Enter your serial number" is a prompt. Think of it as a mini print( ) function. However, the actual print( ) function has more capabilities and you can't use print( ) within the input( ) function.

Try the following code in immediate mode:

```
>>> x = input(print("this is wrong")
... asdf
  File "<stdin>", line 2
    asdf
       ^
SyntaxError: invalid syntax
```

Note that in the code above, the input function will still wait for any text that the user will enter. That is why there is a line of ellipses after the input statement. I then entered "asdf".

After that Python gave an error message. Again, you can't use the print( ) function inside the input( ) function. That is why the print( ) function's syntax already has an argument in it called "prompt".

So, here's how the input( ) function works. When the function is executed by the program, it will display the text inside the prompt first. The entire program will then pause.

It will only continue after the user has entered something. Whatever is entered using the keyboard will be stored in the identifier "x". You can then use the statement print(x) to display the value contained in that variable.

In the next chapter we will go over what variables are in Python programming and we will also gloss over what comments are in this programming language.

## Key Takeaways:

- Keywords like input and print can't be used as identifiers
- Identifiers are names given to program structures in Python and they are used to distinctly identify one from the other
- Identifiers have syntax rules like they can't start with numbers and symbols aren't allowed (except for the underscore "_" )
- Identifiers are case sensitive. That means even if two identifiers look almost alike with just one having a single capital letter and other one doesn't—when that happens, these identifiers will be treated as two separate and distinct variables.

# Chapter 4: Variables and Operators

At the end of the previous chapter, we began using another term called "variables." If you're thinking that this lesson is starting to look like physics or some kind of math, then you're right!

Well, not exactly.

Yes, we will do some math, but not just math. You probably remember variables from your very first algebra class. Well, that's almost the same in Python programming but still a bit different.

## What's a Variable?

The makers of Python made everything quite descriptive so that the code itself is very easy to understand. The same goes for the non-code stuff in this language—like variables. You won't see the word "variable" in the list of keywords in the previous chapter.

That means you can use it as an identifier!

However, going back to our discussion, a variable in the Python programming language is a kind of container that holds a certain value. These containers don't have to hold a specific kind of value. In fact, you can change the contents of each of these containers or variables.

This is a programming concept in Python and other languages that may want to learn in the future.

However, going a bit techie on the subject, when you add a variable in your code, what you're actually telling the computer to do is to reserve or allocate a portion of its random access memory for storing data that you will use later on. In this sense, a variable is a container of sorts.

## Quick Programming Exercise

To help you understand variables better, here's a little programming exercise.

1. Pull up immediate mode in Python
2. Type the following code: x = 123
3. Now, print x (remember, it is case sensitive)
4. Next, type the following code y = "hey you!"
5. Now, print y
6. Next, type the following line of code: x = y
7. Now, print x
8. And then print y
9. What's the final value of these two variables?

## What We Can Learn from That Exercise

There are several things that we can learn from the above exercise. First off, is that you can assign both numbers and letters or even alphanumeric values to variables.

The next important thing that you will learn here is that there is no need for variable declarations in Python.

**What is a Variable Declaration?** A variable declaration is a statement or line of code usually at the beginning of a program that creates variables that will be used later in the program.

Python does not require you to use variable declarations and you can create a variable anytime and anywhere as needed in your program code. In the world of programming, Python is called a type-inferred language. It already identifies the type of variable for you (i.e. characters, integers, real numbers, Boolean etc.).

You can use the print( ) function to display the value of a variable. An example of that is this line:

```
>>> print(x)
```

In that example, you just need to put the variable "x" inside the print( ) function and it will serve as the argument for that function. Again, as it was mentioned earlier, this function has a lot of capabilities besides displaying text on the screen.

Another thing that we can learn from the above exercise is that you use the equal sign ("=") to assign values to variables – just like you do in algebra. So, typing "x = 25" will assign the numeric value 25 to the variable x. You can then print x to see its value.

The equal sign is called an operator in programming—i.e. the assignment operator. There are other operators other than this one. We'll cover that in a later section of this book.

You don't need to use multiple lines of code to assign values to different variables in Python programming. You can create and assign values to the variables using just one line of code.

You just need to separate the variables and their corresponding values with comas.

Here's an example:

```
>>> a, b, c = 5, 3.2, "Hello"
>>> print(a)
5
>>> print(b)
3.2
>>> print(c)
Hello
>>>
```

Try that in immediate mode and see if you get the same results. You can also use the same principle when you want to assign the same value to the multiple variables. Here is another example:

```
>>> a = b = c = 21
>>> print(a)
21
>>> print(b)
21
>>> print(c)
21
>>>
```

You can use other operators to change the value contained in a variable. But that will be for later. For now, just remember that the assignment operator "=" is the one you use to assign values to variables.

## Types of Variables

As it was mentioned earlier, a variable may contain different data types. You already know that variables in Python can contain numbers and letters in them. However, they can actually contain other types of data other than those two.

Remember that one of the biggest applications of this programming language is in data science and artificial intelligence. That means there are actually more data types that you will learn as you master Python.

The five standard data types that you should know about include the following:

- Numbers
- Dictionary
- String
- Tuple
- List

Numbers in Python Programming

When we say numbers in Python programming we refer to different kinds of numeric data. There are four different types of numbers or numeric data in this programming language.

They include the following:

1.  Integer or int – these are whole numbers whether they are negative or positive
2.  Long – these are long integers and they can be represented in hexadecimal and octal formats
3.  Float – these include any real numbers or any number with a fractional part
4.  Complex numbers

Integers in Python include numbers like 10, -700, 080, -40, 0x69, and -0x200.

Examples of long numbers are 0xEFABCECBDAE, 24361L, and -052735L. Python always uses a capital "L" for long numbers, which helps you distinguish that letter from the number 1—i.e. if you use the small "L" it would look like a 1 on the screen.

**HINT**: always use the big L when writing long numbers in your programming code.

Floating point numbers in this language include numbers such as 0.2, 15.5, 0.0, -80.0, -32.15e100, -2.5, and 70.6-E12.

Examples of complex numbers include 4.53e-7j, 54.j, 3e+26J, and 9.322e-36j. Remember that in Python, a complex number is represented by two real numbers in an ordered pair. It follows the pattern x + yj—x and y in this equation are the real numbers and j denotes the imaginary numerical unit.

## Strings, Words, and Characters

Other than numbers, you have also used single characters and words and alphanumeric strings in our exercises. You can use them as values for a type of variable called a string. Strings in Python refer to any contiguous set characters. This includes single letters or a combination of numbers.

To identify a string in this language is by using a pair of quotation marks. You can use either single quotes or double quotes. This means if you enclose a number in double or single quotes and assign that as the value of a variable then it is treated as a string and not a number.

Take a look at the following example:

```
>>> sample = "1"
>>> sample + 1
Traceback (most recent call last):
  File "<stdin>", line 1, in <module>
TypeError: can only concatenate str (not "int") to str
>>> sample = 1
>>> sample + 1
2
>>>
```

In the example above, the variable sample is first assigned a string i.e. "1". It is treated as a string not as a number. That is why when you try to add a +1 (i.e. a number) to the variable called sample, it produces an error – you can't add a numeric value to a string value.

However, if you look at the next couple of lines, you will see that the same variable is now assigned a numeric value of 1. When you add +1 to that variable (i.e. sample + 1) then there is no error produced and the result of the operation is displayed, which is 2, on the next line.

## Manipulating Contiguous Strings

We mentioned earlier that strings in this programming language are actually treated as a contiguous set of characters. Since they are sets, then there should be a way to access subsets of a string just like you do in math. You can do that in Python by using the [ ] known as the slice operator.

The slice operator also uses a colon in between [ : ] to separate between the different indices such as [0:3] etc. Please do the exercise below to help you understand related programming principles.

## Programming Exercise

Try the following sample code in immediate mode:

```
>>> str = "abcde"
>>> print(str[0])
a
>>> print(str[1])
b
>>> print(str[2])
c
>>> print(str[3])
d
>>> print(str[4])
e
```

From this exercise we learn that the first character in a string is referenced with [0] index and the others follow suit in the series. That means the second index (or character) is accessed by [1], the third with a [2], and so on.

If you want to print the first letter of the string in the variable called var, you will use [0] to print the letter "a".

If you want to add more characters to a string, then you should use the + operator and if you want to repeat the string at its full length use the * operator.

Check out the following example:

```
>>> print(str + "fghij")
abcdefghij
>>> print(str * 2)
abcdeabcde
>>>
```

## Selecting Subsets of Strings

As it was explained earlier, you can also use the slice [ ] operator to refer to a subset of a string. You will use colon (i.e. ":") to refer to the start of the subset and the end of the subset of the entire index.

Using the same example in the previous exercise, we will assign the value of "abcde" to the variable called str using this statement:

>>> str = "abcde"

To print only the third to the fifth character in that string, use this line:

>>> print(str[2:5])

To print everything from the second character to the last one, use the following line:

>>> print(str[1:])

## Programming Exercise

1. Assign the value "abcdefghij" to the variable var1.
2. Create another variable called var2 and let it have the same value as var1 except for its first 3 letters.

3. Print var2

Note that you will see the answers to this exercise after the key takeaways section of this chapter.

## Key Takeaways

- A variable represents a memory allocation where certain values are stored
- There are basic variable types in Python and each one is treated differently
- You use operators to assign and alter the values contained in variables
- You use variables in the input( ) function
- When numbers are enclosed in quotation marks they are treated as strings not numbers.

Answer to the last exercise:

```
>>> var1 = "abcdefghij"
>>> var2 = var1[3:]
>>> print(var2)
defghij
>>>
```

# Chapter 5: More Variables and More Operators

We have gone over the first two types of variables that you are already familiar with—numbers and letters/words. In this chapter we will go over some more variables that are unique to programming that you may not be familiar with namely lists, tuples, and dictionaries. We will also go over other operators as well.

## List Data in Python Programming

Another type of variable in Python is called a list. A list is exactly what its namesake means—it's a list of things. List data doesn't have to be of the same type. That means that some items on a list may be numbers and some items can be numbers among others.

The items in a list should be contained within a pair of square brackets and the items are separated by commas. Here is a sample list created in Python code:

```
>>> mylist = [123, "abc", "Henry James", "221b Baker Street"]
```

As you can see in the example above, we're also using the [ ] operator for lists. The same rules apply if you want to access and change the values within a list.

So, if you want to print the contents of the entire list, you can use the following line for our sample list above:

```
>>> print(mylist)
```

If you want to print the first item in the list above, use this line:

```
>>> print(mylist[0])
```

If you want to display the second item to the four item on the list use this line:

```
>>> print(mylist[1:4])
```

If you want to print only the 3rd and 4th items on the list use the following line:

```
>>> print(mylist[2:4])
```

If you want to display the 2nd and 4th items on this list, use the following:

```
>>> print(mylist[1], mylist[3])
```

If you want to print the entire list twice, use the * operator (this is the operator for multiplication).

```
>>> print(mylist * 2)
```

Let's say we created a second called mylist2 with the following values:

```
>>> mylist2 = [98, 76, 54, 32, 1]
```

You can combine mylist and mylist2 by using the + sign. See the following sample:

```
>>> print(mylist + mylist2)
```

Programming Exercise

1. Create a list containing 3 names of people in it.
2. Create a second list that contains 3 phone numbers.
3. Print the first items from both lists.
4. Print the second name from the first list and the first phone number from the second list.
5. Print the third name from the first list and the third name from the second list.
6. Print "Hello!" on one line followed by "Nice to meet you" on the second line and then insert one of the names from the first list on the second line.

## Tuples

Tuples are another sequential data type in Python and are very similar to list data in almost every same way. The big difference between a list and a tuple in Python is that you can alter the data contained in a list but you can't change the data in a tuple once it is created.

To help you differentiate a list from a tuple in this programming language, you will use a pair of parenthesis for tuples instead of square brackets, which is what is used for lists.

The following is an example of a tuple:

```
>>> mytuple = (123, "abc", "Henry James", "221b Baker Street")
```

You also use the slice operator to access the items in your tuple. So, let's say we want to access the last data in mytuple above, you will use the following line:

```
>>> print(mytuple[3])
```

Notice that it looks almost the same as accessing data on lists. Of course, again, the difference is in the fact that you can't alter the data contained in tuples and you can only access and print them.

Remember that you use the slice indicator to refer to every index on a tuple as you would a list. Please refer to the samples earlier (the ones we used for lists in Python) regarding how to use a slice operator.

## Dictionaries

Think of dictionaries as some kind of hash table. They are composed of two elements:

1. The key
2. The value

Just like the list and the tuple, dictionaries can be of any data type in this programming language. You can use numbers and string data either as the key or the value.

Here is an example of a dictionary:

mydictionary = {1 : 'this is the value of the key called one'}

This line of code creates the dictionary called mydictionary. In this example, the number 1 here is the key and the string after the colon 'this is the value of the key called one' is the value of the dictionary.

Think of this as some kind of actual dictionary. The item on the left of the colon is the term and the item on the right after the colon is the explanation of the term on the left as it were—we're just trying to draw parallels here.

So, if you're looking for the "definition" (figuratively speaking) of 1 in mydictionary, you just need to print or access it by using the index called "1". Here's an example that I want you to try in immediate mode.

```
>>>
>>> mydictionary = {1 : 'this is the value of the key called one'}
>>>
>>> print(mydictionary[1])
this is the value of the key called one
>>>
```

As you can see, you use the slice operator to access the value of the key called 1 in this dictionary. You can add more keys and values to mydictionary by just declaring them as needed in your program code using the slice operator as well.

Here is an example of how you can do that:

>>> mydictionary['second'] = 'this is the value for the key called second'

Now, having created a second key and value, if you print mydictionary, it would now look like this:

```
>>>
{1: 'this is the value of the key called one', 'second': 'this is the value for the key called second'}
>>> print(mydictionary)
>>>
>>> mydictionary['second'] = 'this is the value for the key called second'
```

From the example above, we can see that:

- A second key and value pair was added on the first line
- You can use a string as the key and also a string as the value. You can actually use either of the two as key or value. For instance, you can create a third key and value pair like this: mydictionary[3] = 3 and it will work perfectly and you will be adding a third key-value pair to that dictionary.

52

- You can access any of the values in your dictionary by using the key data as your index.
- You can print the entire dictionary by using the print( ) function.

## It's Time to Operate!

We have already introduced you to a number of operators in Python. You have used the assignment operator, the slice operator, and numeric operators as well. In this section of this chapter we will go over the operators and what they can do to change the values that are contained in the variables that you will create.

The following are the different types of operators used in the Python programming language:

- Math operators
- Logical operators
- Assignment operators
- Relational or comparison operators
- Membership operators
- Bitwise operators
- Identity operators

For the purposes of this introductory book to programming principles and the Python programming language, you will mostly be using math, logical, assignment, and relational operators.

But that doesn't mean you shouldn't know about the other operators mentioned in that list. For this reason, We will just focus on the most basic ones that you will use for now and then just explain the rest so you can have a framework with which you can continue as you learn more about the principles of programming.

Math Operators in Python

Math operators are probably the easiest ones to understand simply because you're already familiar with them. We use a few slightly different symbols in programming simply because some of the symbols have a different meaning in the computer world.

For instance the math symbols for multiplication and division are the × (multiplication) and ÷ (division) symbols respectively. Notice that you don't have both keys on your keyboard. You don't have the division symbol right on your standard QWERTY keyboard.

You may have an 'x' on your keyboard but that isn't exactly the symbol for multiplication. FYI, there is a specific ASCII code for producing the multiplication symbol.

- *Multiplication symbol*

The symbol for multiplication is the asterisk "*" and you will find that it is the standard in pretty much any other programming language. In fact, if you launch the calculator in Windows 10, you invoke multiplication when you press the asterisk on your numeric keypad.

- *Division*

The division symbol on Python programming (and other languages as well) is the forward slash "/" – and that is the same thing you will use on your numeric keypad as well.

- *Addition*

This one is easy—it's the + sign—readily available on your keyboard.

- *Subtraction*

This one is easy as well; it's the minus sign "-" and it's right on your keyboard too.

- *Modulus*

If you want to divide one number for the other and you're only interested in getting the remainder of the division operation, then use the "%" symbol (i.e. modulus) to get that.

- *Floor division*

If you're not interested in getting the decimal values after a division operation or if you want the result rounded off away from zero then use the floor division symbol, which is "//" the double forward slash.

- *Exponent*

The symbol used in Python for getting the exponent is a double asterisk "**". For example, 3 to the power of 2 is written as 3**2, and the result of course is 9.

Assignment Operators

You already know one type of assignment operator in Python programming. It's the "=". As a kind of review, the value to the right of this symbol will be assigned to the variable at the left of this symbol.

For instance, if you encode this line:

>>> x = 10

If you print the value of x in that statement, it will return a 10. But that is not the only assignment operator in this programming language. Let's run down on that quickly. Note that these assignment operators are pretty much easy to understand when you see the symbols themselves:

| | | |
|---|---|---|
| += | Adds the value of the variable on the left to the one on the right and assigns the sum to the variable on the left of the operator | e.g. A += B is the same as A = A + B |
| -= | Subtracts the value of the variable on the right to the value of the one on the left and then assigns the difference to the variable on the left. | e.g. A -= B is the same as A = A - B |
| *= | Multiplies the value of the two variables and then assigns the product to the variable at the left | e.g. A *= B is the equivalent of A = A * B |

| | | |
|---|---|---|
| /= | Divides the value of the variable on the left of the operator by the value of the variable to the right of the operator and then assigns the quotient to the variable to the left of the operator. | e.g. A /= B is the equivalent of A = A / B |
| %= | Does a modulus operation of the two values and then assigns the remainder to the variable to the left of the operator | e.g. A %= B is the equivalent of A = A % B |
| **= | Computes the exponent of the base number on the left by the number on the right and then the result is assigned to the variable to the left of the operator | e.g. A **= B is the equivalent of A = A ** B |
| //= | Does a floor division of the two variables/values and then assigns the value of the quotient to the variable to the left of the operator | e.g. A //= B is the equivalent of A = A // B |

## Comparison/Relational Operators

This is another easy set of operators in Python programming simply because we all have been comparing values since we were little. It's just that in programming, we use some slightly different symbols than what we used to have in math.

Comparison operators are used to test whether a condition in a given equation is either true or false. These operators will become very useful when we get to the part where you need to add some decision making capabilities to your computer program.

| | |
|---|---|
| == | This is the equal to sign. The condition is true if both the values on either side of the operator are equal |
| != | This is also known as the not equal to sign. The condition is true if the values to either side are not equal |
| <> | This is similar to the not equal to operator |
| > | This is the greater than symbol. For this condition to return true, the value on the left of the operator should be greater than the value to the right |
| | This is known as the less than operator. This condition returns |

| | |
|---|---|
| < | true if the value to the left is less than the one to the right of the operator |
| >= | This is also known as the greater than or equal to operator. The condition will be true if the value to the left is greater than or equal to the one to the right of the operator. |
| <= | This is known as the less than or equal to operator. This will return true if the value to its left is less than or equal to the value to its right side. |

Logical Operators

Python also supports logical operators that can be used to test conditions. They include the following:

- and – known as the logical and operator. If condition A and condition B are true (e.g. test1 and test2) then this operation returns true.
- or – known as the logical or operator. It only requires either of the two conditions to be true to return a value of true.
- not – known as the logical not operator (e.g. not(A and B)). The function of this operator is to reverse result of the original operand.

Membership Operators

You will use membership operators to test whether a certain value belongs to a particular sequence like in a list, tuple, or string. There are only 2 membership operators in Python, which include the following:

- in – this operator returns true if the value/variable to the left is within the sequence at the right (e.g. 2 in serial_number, x in y, 'Baker Street' in _streetAddress, q in Alphabet)
- not in – this is the opposite of the in-operator. It returns true if the value to the left is not within the sequence on the right.

Bitwise Operators

Python also supports bitwise operations, which include the following:

- & (binary AND operator) – copies a bit result if it is existing in both of the operands in an expression.
- | (binary OR operator) – copies a bit if it exists in either of the two operands.
- ^ (binary XOR operator) – copies a bit if it exists in one of the operands but not found in the other.
- ~ (ones complement) – flips the bits.

- << (left shift operator) – shifts the value of the operand going to the left as specified by the value to the right of this operator.
- >> (right shift operator) – shifts the value of the operand going to the right according to the value to the right of this operator

## Identity Operators

These operators are used to check the memory locations of objects. There are only two of these operators:

- is – this operator will return true if the two variables being compared are actually pointing to the same object
- is not – the opposite of the previous operator. It will return true if the two variables being compared aren't pointing to the same object.

## More Math Rules

In mathematics we have operator precedence. A useful mnemonic is MDAS, which is a rule that means whenever you have a series of math operations in one expression, you will first perform multiplication, followed by division, and then addition, and lastly subtraction ergo the MDAS rule.

There is also precedence in the many operators that we have mentioned here in this chapter. No, you don't need to memorize a horrendous order of different operators. The precedence in this programming language isn't that complicated but it will need some effort to remember the precedence.

Please go over the following list (no there won't be a quiz later—big grin!). This lists the precedence from first to last.

1. Exponentiation
2. Complements, unary plus and minus
3. Multiplication
4. Division, modulus, floor division (they're all in the same level)
5. Addition
6. Subtraction
7. Right and left bitwise shifts
8. Bitwise and
9. Bitwise or
10. All comparison operators
11. All of the equality operators
12. Assignment operators
13. All identity operators
14. Membership
15. Logical operators

**Programming Exercises**

1. Write an programming expression that will compute and print the average of three numbers
2. Create a list that has 7 phone numbers. Print the 3rd phone number in that list.
3. Prompt a user to input a number from 1 to 10. Assign that number to a variable. After that, test whether the number that the user entered is odd or even. Finally, write a statement that will display on screen whether the number that was entered was odd or even.

Key Takeaways

- The list variable type is literally a list of things that you can manipulate just like a contiguous set of any type of data.
- Dictionaries and tuples are like lists but with slightly different properties
- A tuple is like a list but you can't modify its contents
- A dictionary is a list of key-value pairs.
- You access the value of a dictionary by using the key as your index
- You can add more key-value pairs to a dictionary using the slice operator
- Math operators in Python look almost exactly like the ones we use in math except for the multiplication, division, and exponentiation.

- You can use logical, comparison, and other operators to test conditions, which allows your program to do some decision making processes.
- Operators in Python follow a precedence

# Chapter 6: It's Time to Get IDLE and Put It All Together

In all of the pop quizzes, programming exercises, and other bits of coding that we have done so far, you have been working with Python's immediate mode. Essentially what you've been doing is giving single line commands and then Python will execute that line of command.

After that you will enter another command and then the computer will be programming to do that single line of code. In this chapter we will take things a step further—you will write code detailing tasks one step at a time and your computer will do whatever is encoded in continuous steps until everything is completed.

In short, you don't need to type one line of command after the other.

## Using IDLE

IDLE is short for Integrated Development and Learning Environment. As it was explained earlier, it is an integrated development environment (IDE). This is your primary tool for building programming projects in Python.

Immediate mode gives you the advantage of testing the lines of code immediately to see if your syntax works. However, using IDLE (and other IDEs) will give you a few more benefits that you won't get with the black screen.

Here are some of those benefits:

- *It allows you save your work and update your files*: IDEs allow you to create a program file, add lines of code to it, save it even if you're not done, and come back some time later to continue working on your program.

- *It allows you to debug your work*: debugging refers to the act of fixing programming errors. Mistakes in the code tend to happen from time to time and it will be very difficult to spot mistakes manually especially if you're dealing with hundreds of lines of code when you're developing apps.

- *It allows you to run your program within the programming environment*: you can test your code without the need for letting your program go live. This means you can test how well your app is coming along even though it's not yet complete.

- *IDEs can highlight the syntax of your program code*: this feature allows you to spot which part of your code requires a certain level of syntax while separating the variables and other user-defined portions of your program.

- *Automatic code formatting*: IDEs that support Python can automatically format your code, which makes writing your programs a lot easier.

There are other useful features as well, but these are the top benefits that you can get from an integrated development environment.


Launching IDLE

Launching IDLE is easy. You just type IDLE in the search box, if you're using Windows 10, like this:

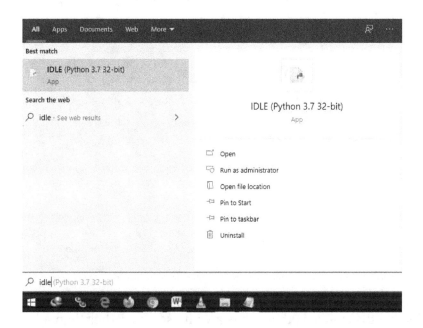

To launch IDLE in Linux, click Menu and then the terminal icon and then enter IDLE (or IDLE3 or whatever version of Python you have installed on your computer). And then that will launch the Python shell.

When you hit enter (or its equivalent on your OS), then you will see a screen that looks kind of like this:

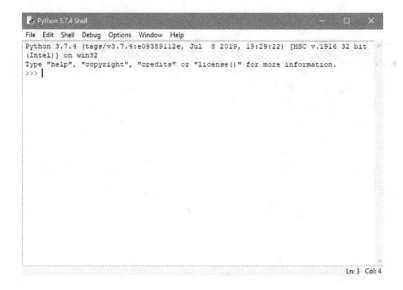

This is the Python shell and it behaves just like immediate mode. The big difference is that it has a white screen rather than a black one.

Both the shell and immediate mode will wait for a line of programming code. Once you enter a complete line of code it will execute the code or perform the command that you entered.

And then once the command has been accomplished it all loops back to the beginning and it is going to wait for the next code that you will enter.

Using the IDLE Text Editor

An IDE like IDLE will come with its own text editor. That means you don't need MS Word, Notepad, Notepad++, or some other text

68

editor. To launch the built-in text editor, go to File and then select New File on the menu at the top of the shell window.

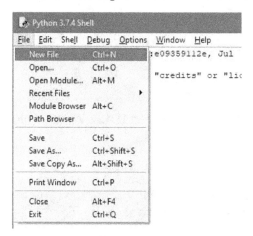

Doing that will open a text editor window that looks kind of like this one:

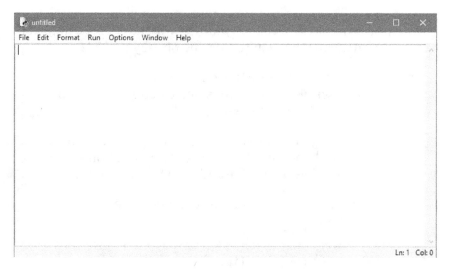

Note that your editor window may look a bit different than that one since yours may already be the most recent update. Notice that this new file is called "untitled" which you can see at the top left of the window.

## Programming Exercise—Creating and Opening a New File in IDLE

This time, let's create a new file in IDLE. We then close that file and then open it. Here are the steps:

1. In the editor window, go to File > Save As...

2. In the window that will pop up, navigate to and select the folder where you want to save the file.

3. Type a new name for that file—call it "My First Python Program"

4. You will then see the name that you typed on the top left of that window. Notice that your file will have a .py extension, which means that you're working on a Python file.

5. Now, click the red X on the top right of the window and close that Python file. Alternatively you can do an Alt-F4 or go to File > Close from the menu.

6. After closing that file, you can open it by going to File on the menu and then navigate to the folder where you saved your file earlier. Select your file and then hit the enter key.

7. This will open the file you just created earlier.

## Writing Your First Code in IDLE

Now that you know how to create and open a Python file, it's time to add some code into it. Create a file called First Python Program.py. After that, type the following print statements in that window:

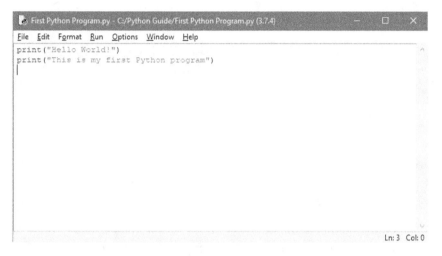

After typing those two lines, save your work. And then this is you can run this program within the Python environment:

1. Click Run from the menu

2. Click on Run Module

3. That will bring up the Python shell.

4. It will display the following screen.

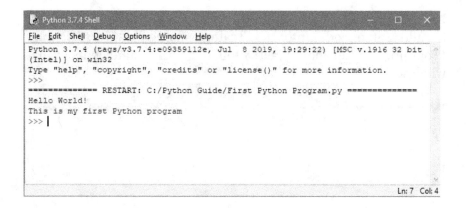

Notice that the Shell window did not display the print( ) statement, but it just displayed exactly what was supposed to be shown on the screen, which are the texts that were inside the print statements.

Now you know how to create a Python program file, how to open these file types, how to edit these files, and how to run the program that you just created.

Notice that your first Python program file only has two lines of code and you didn't need to press the enter key for each command line just like you previously did in Python's immediate mode.

Well, this time you're now creating program files that will later be developed into Python apps.

Programming Exercise

1.  Create a new Python file. You get to choose what to name it.

2. Print "Hello world!" in one line.

3. Next, print each letter on its own line

4. Run this file.

5. Create a new Python file. Name it as the "Hi, What's Your Name?" file

6. In this next file print "Hello World!"

7. Next, ask for user input using the prompt "Hi, what's your name?"

8. Save the user's answer in a variable called response1

9. In the next line print "Hi, " followed by the user's name, and finally "Nice to meet you!"

10. Run this file.

11. Add another line that will print "That's it. Bye bye"

12. Save and run this edited file

You will find the answers to this programming exercise at the end of this chapter. Note that you should have created 2 Python files by the end of this exercise.

## Key Takeaways

- IDLE allows you to create actual Python files that can later be exported into actual apps and programs that can be installed and run on your computer and other supporting devices.

- IDEs have a lot of advantages over just using immediate mode.

- You can debug as you go and your IDE will flag any mistakes in your code.

- All the programming statements that you need can be encoded and then executed using an IDE such as IDLE.

**Answers to Programming Exercises:**

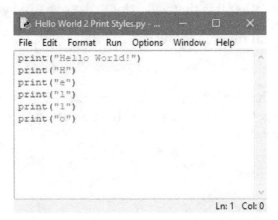

File   Edit   Format   Run   Options   Window   Help

```
print("Hello World!")
name1 = input("Hi, what's your name?")
print("Hi, ", name1, "Nice to meet you!")
```

Ln: 3   Col: 41

# Chapter 7: Making Decisions

In an earlier chapter, we mentioned that some variables and operators are necessary for making decisions within a Python program. Here's an example:

1.  You ask for the user's name and password.

2.  You then check if the name and password matches

3.  If it matches then the user is logged into the system.

4.  If the name and password don't match, then provide an error message.

What you know so far is how to display messages in different ways, different types of variables at your disposal, and how to take input from users. The next step is to know how to interpret the user input and change the response of the program depending on the user's input.

## The If Statement

To allow for decision making in programming, there should be conditional statements apart from statements that output data to the screen or input data from the keyboard (or some other input device like a mouse or a touch screen).

The IF-statement in Python allows you to do just that.

It's very easy to understand, really. This statement will evaluate a condition whether it is true or false. If the condition is true then one action will be taken. If the condition is false then a different action will be taken—just like in the four-step password decision we mentioned earlier.

Here's an example of an if-statement in Python.

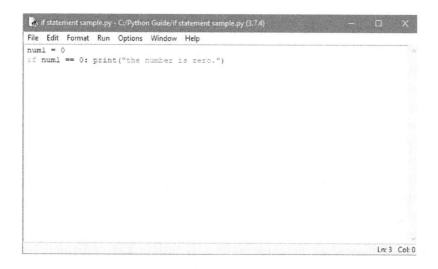

Type those lines in IDLE and run it. In this example, we assigned the value zero to the variable num1. We then use a condition to test whether num1 has a zero or not. If it does then it prints text confirming that the value is indeed zero.

This is an if-statement that has only one action. If num1 doesn't have zero, then the program will do nothing. To create two different potential actions within an if-statement, then we add an else line to that statement.

Take a look at the following example:

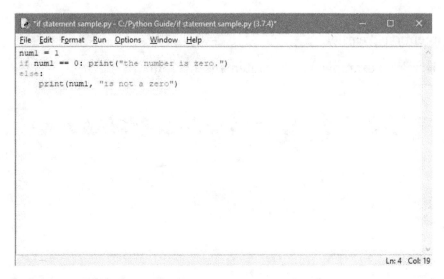

```
num1 = 1
if num1 == 0: print("the number is zero.")
else:
    print(num1, "is not a zero")
```

Ln: 4  Col: 19

Run that on IDLE and check out the results. As you will see, this program will execute the second print statement instead of the first one since the variable num1 does not contain a zero.

In this example we have two potential actions that your program can take depending on the value of the variable num1.

Now, Python allows you to have more than 2 branches in this decision. You can do that by adding an elif-line to the program that you already have.

See the following example of an if- elif- else-statement:

```
num1 = -2
if num1 == 0:
    print("the number is zero.")
elif num1 > 0:
    print(num1, "is positive.")
else:
    print(num1, "is negative")
```

In this third example, we have a program that will check whether the variable num1 contains a positive number, a negative number, or a zero. Notice the comparison operators that were used.

What do you think will be displayed on the screen?

Programming Exercises

- Write a program that will ask for any number from 1 to 10.

- Let the program decide if the number that was entered was a zero, a positive number, or a negative number.

- Print the appropriate response to the screen.

- Write another program that is almost similar to the first one. This time, it should display whether the number that was entered was either an odd or even number.


Key Takeaways
- The If-statement plus comparison, logical, and other operators allow decision making in Python programs

- The If-statement allows you to branch the program flow to two or more actions depending on the conditions in the decision making process

- You can add an else- and elif- to an if-statement to create different courses of action

# Chapter 8: Algorithms and Commenting

Now that you're working with multiple lines of code, we can introduce you to a new programming concept called algorithms. Formulating an algorithm will help you break down big programming projects into smaller sections that logically produce the desired solution.

> **What is an algorithm?** In computer programming, an algorithm is like a formula or a recipe. It refers to a sequence of specific instructions that a computer should perform in order to produce the desired result.

## How Do You Fry an Egg?

Remember that an algorithm is like a recipe. This means that there are certain steps and each step is a prerequisite for the next step. That means you can't just mix up the sequence of steps or else you will mess things up.

Here's an easy exercise. Try to answer this simple question:

*How do you fry an egg? Teach me as if I have never cooked anything before in my life.*

Think about that for a minute. Let's say you were teaching your kid how to fry something for the very first time. How would you explain the process to that child well enough that no mistakes will be committed?

Here's one potential way to do it:

1. Get a regular bowl, an egg, and a fork.

2. Place the bowl on the table, take the egg in one hand, and crack it with the fork. Don't crack it too much that the insides spill. Put the fork down on the table.

3. Open the egg above the bowl splitting the shell into two pieces. Let the yolk and the egg white fall into the bowl. Throw the shell in the trash.

4. Sprinkle a pinch of salt and pepper on the egg.

5. Grab your fork and mix everything in the bowl. Make sure everything is mixed well.

6. Grab a non-stick pan and put it on the stove. Turn the stove on to heat the pan. Add a little oil into the pan. Let the pan heat up for about a minute.

7. Grab your beaten egg and pour the mixture slowly into the hot pan. Set the bowl aside. Wait for the egg to get nice and firm.

8. Grab a spatula and jab it under the egg and lift it up and over turning it bottom side up.

9. Turn the heat off the pan.

10. Grab a plate. Using your spatula, take the egg from off the pan and then put it on the center of the plate.

11. You can now eat your scrambled egg.

From this example, we know that we can't skip a step and still get the same result—i.e. a properly scrambled and cooked egg. You also can't switch steps. You can't hope to cook an egg by tossing it into the pan, cracking it open, and then putting it in the bowl and then heating the pan later.

## Ticketing Software

The same is true with the Python programs that you will make. The instructions you will give should be arranged in a logical and chronological order. Here's an example of an algorithm for a ticketing software program.

**Problem:** create a ticketing software program that will check if a visitor's ticket is valid or not. You will know that it is valid if the serial number is in a list of official ticket serial numbers.

**Solution:** here is an algorithm that may be able to solve the problem.

1. Create a list of official serial numbers and store it in a variable.

2. Ask the visitor to enter the serial number found on their ticket and store that in another variable.

3. Query the list using the serial number that was provided by the customer.

4. If the customer provided a serial number that is in your list then allow them to enter.

5. If not, then ask for a valid serial number but don't let the visitor inside the premises.

Note that we haven't written any Python code yet. However, as you go over each step in that algorithm, may already have thought of the Python functions and statements that you will need to write that part of the computer program.

Think of an algorithm as a plan or pattern that you will use to compose your Python program. You will need algorithms for very large projects and apps. For example, an app on your phone will require a long and detailed algorithm to make sure there are no flaws in your logical steps.

Algorithms give you a definite path that will ensure that the program code that you will write is efficient and bug-proof.

## Programming Exercises

1. Write a detailed algorithm that will teach someone who will be using a stapler for the very first time.

2. Write an algorithm that will teach someone how to draw a simple smiley face using a paper and pencil.

3. Create an algorithm that searches for a student's student number

## Comments and Annotating Your Programs

Just like other programming languages, Python allows users to put comments on their code. These comments are used to annotate your programming work.

Think of comments as side notes on your code that will help you and others to figure out what purpose each part of your code is supposed to fulfill. This makes app/program development to run a lot smoother.

To add a comment on any Python code, all you need to do is to put a hash symbol/mark before typing anything else. You can even turn an entire line of code into a comment.

Try the following on IDLE and see which line gets printed:

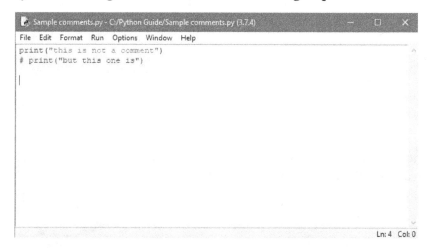

The first line will display on the screen but the second one won't. Note that in IDLE comments are in red while the other parts like reserved words, text, arguments, and others will have a different color.

Comments are intended for you not for IDLE's compiler. That means any comment in your code will be ignored and skipped.

> **What is a compiler?** A compiler is a piece of software that is built into an IDE that converts your program code into machine readable instructions.

85

**BIG TIP:** Make your comments descriptive. Tell the reader (i.e. people who will be looking at your code) what each part is supposed to do. Check out the following example:

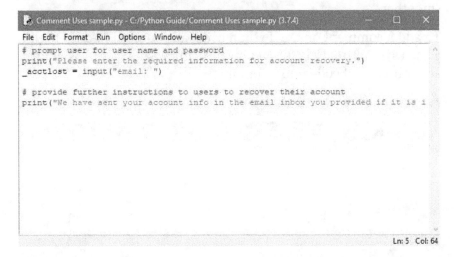

The comments are short and concise yet they provide you with an idea of what each part of the code does.

Key Takeaways

- Algorithms allow you to design your program code efficiently. They should be logically arranged and they can be as specific or as general as you want them to be.

- Comments allow you to annotate your work so that everyone in your team will know what each part of the code is supposed to do.

# Chapter 9: Loops

There will be plenty of times when you need to repeat certain actions over and over. You may need to display certain messages to the screen over and over, you may have to perform calculations over and over, and you may have to ask the info from users until they give you the right one etc.

If you type the same lines of code over and over just to make that repeating effect, then your program code will tend to get longer than necessary. The good news is that Python allows you reiterate certain steps so you don't have to type them again and again.

To do that, you need to use loops or looping functions.

> **What is a Loop?** A loop in programming reiterates a specified code over and over until a given condition is fulfilled. For instance, your code can ask for the right password over and over until the user supplies the right one.

There are two loops in Python—the for-loop and the while loop.

## The For-Loop

The for-loop allows you to specify the number of times an action (or actions) should be repeated. The only way to stop the reiteration is by fulfilling a certain condition inside the loop or when the number of times you have specified has been reached.

The number of reiterations doesn't necessarily have to be numeric like 1 to 10 times for example. You can use the number of items in a string, list, or even a tuple.

For instance, you have 12 items in your tuple, you can run the for-loop until all the items in the sequence have been used. *FYI:* This type of reiteration is called a traversal in the world of programming.

The for-loop starts with the keyword "for" followed by a variable that you will specify. It will then be followed by the reserved word "in" and then a sequence, which can be a number, tuple, list, string, etc.

The syntax of this loop will look like this:

**for** [variable] **in** [sequence] **:**

**Body of for-loop**

Take note of the required syntax and the indentations used. Let's go over a programming exercise to help you understand how a for-loop works.

Programming Exercise

Let's say a user already provided a series of numbers and it was already stored in a list variable called "any_1". What you need to provide the user is the sum of all of the numbers that the user has supplied. You store the sum in a variable called "sum_1".

Here is a sample code that will add up all the numbers using a for-loop. Try it on IDLE and see what output you're going to get.

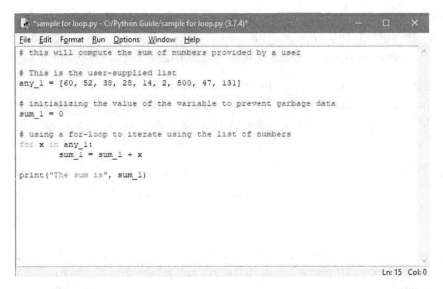

```
📝 *sample for loop.py - C:/Python Guide/sample for loop.py (3.7.4)*     —   □   ✕

File  Edit  Format  Run  Options  Window  Help
# this will compute the sum of numbers provided by a user

# This is the user-supplied list
any_1 = [60, 52, 38, 28, 14, 2, 500, 47, 131]

# initializing the value of the variable to prevent garbage data
sum_1 = 0

# using a for-loop to iterate using the list of numbers
for x in any_1:
        sum_1 = sum_1 + x

print("The sum is", sum_1)




                                                              Ln: 15  Col: 0
```

**BIG TIP:** notice the comments in the sample above? You don't need to annotate every line but if you should at least annotate each important section of your code for future reference.

**ANOTHER BIG TIP:** do you see the comment that says "initializing the value of the variable"? That is a programming best practice. When you create a variable, you need to give it a starting value. Remember that a variable is a memory allocation in your computer's RAM and it is possible that the said memory allocation will have some remaining junk data in it and you don't want that data as the starting value of your variable—it's just going to mess up your math.

Looping Through Numbers

In the previous example, we looped through a list of items (or a list of numbers). But what if you want to use an ascending sequence of

90

numbers, say 1 to 10? To do that you can use the range( ) function. This function will go through numbers from the lowest to the highest.

Here's an example that I want you to try on IDLE:

Note that the above example will print the numbers 0 to 9. The range( ) function starts with zero by default. But you can specify the range of numbers that it will use.

For instance, going back to our example above, if you want the range( ) function to use the numbers 1 to 10 instead of 0 to 9 by default. Instead of using range(10), specify the range as range(1, 11).

This function will use 1 as the start and 11 as the terminating value, which means it will only use up to 10 and then completes its operation once it reaches 11.

Place that range in IDLE and see what numbers get printed.

## Displaying Sequence Contents

Now, moving things up a notch, let's say you don't only want to use numbers but you also want to display and use the items in the list or sequence in a for-loop. To do that, you can use the len( ) function.

The len( ) function determines the number of items within a list, which allows you to index through your sequence.

Try the following sample code to see how the len( ) and range( ) functions work hand in hand.

```
# This program displays items in a grocery list

grocery_list = ['apples', 'potatoes', 'steak', 'coffee']

# iterate through the list using index
for x in range(len(grocery_list)):
        print("Buy some", grocery_list[x])
```

Please run that code on IDLE and see what gets displayed on the screen.

## An Else Block in the For-Loop

The for-loop also allows an else-block to be added to the loop. That last block will be executed after all the items in the sequence have been used. Run the following code in IDLE and see the result:

```
# This program displays items in a grocery list

grocery_list = ['apples', 'potatoes', 'steak', 'coffee']

# iterate through the list using index
for x in range(len(grocery_list)):
        print("Buy some", grocery_list[x])
else:
        print("That's it!")
```

It's pretty much the same program than before, except that we added the else block in the for-loop.

# Side Note: Integer Input

Take note that the input( ) function stores the user's input in string data types. If you try to do math operations with them, then it will produce an error, just like in the following example:

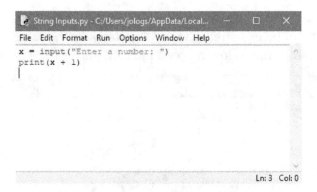

```
x = input("Enter a number: ")
print(x + 1)
```

The above example will return an error if you run it through IDLE.

In order to convert the input from string type to integer so you can do math on the variable that obtained its value with the input( ) function, you need to use the int( ) function to convert the input into an integer type.

In essence you are putting the input( ) function inside the int( ) function. Here's an example:

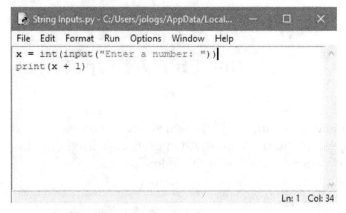

```
x = int(input("Enter a number: "))
print(x + 1)
```

Unlike the original, this updated version will not produce an error.

## The While Loop

As you can see, the for-loop reiterates actions a given number of times. In short, you can determine the number of times the actions are repeated. In contrast, the while-loop will keep reiterating the commands/code in the body as long as a certain condition remains true.

The syntax of this loop looks like this:

**while** [test expression] **:**

**Body of the loop**

Here's an example:

```
x = int(input("Enter a number: "))
y = 1
print("Let's count from 1 to ", x)

while y <= x :
    print(y)
    y += 1
```

Note that you need to increment the value of the test variable within the body of the loop. If it doesn't change, then the loop will virtually run forever. It's either that or the computer runs out of memory.

## Breaking the Continuing the Loop

Speaking of memory dumps and infinite loops, sometimes certain conditions will make the loop run forever even if you write your program code the best you can. The good news is that there are ways to break the loop other than just fulfilling the original conditions that were set.

You can do that by using the "break" statement. By inserting the break statement you terminate the loop immediately regardless of whether the initial condition is true or not.

Here's an example:

```
Sample while loop with break statement.py - C:/Users/jologs/AppData/Local/Programs/Pyth...   —   □   ✕
File  Edit  Format  Run  Options  Window  Help
x = int(input("Enter a number: "))
y = 1
print("Let's count from 1 to ", x)

while y <= x :
  print(y)
  y += 1
  break




|



                                                                        Ln: 12  Col: 0
```

Note that in the above example only the number 1 will be printed to the screen because of the break statement.

Another bit of control flow that you can use in a While-loop is a continue-statement. In contrast to the break statement, a continue-statement will only stop the current iteration.

This makes the flow skip the current iteration but still continue with the rest of the loop.

In the example below, all the numbers will be printed except for the number 3 because of the conditional statement followed by a continue-statement.

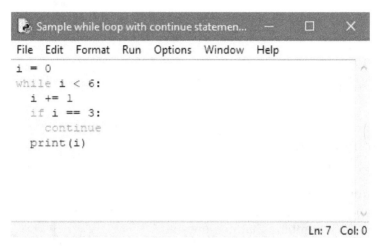

Run that in IDLE and see what happens.

Just like in the for-loop, the while-loop also allows you to use an else-block at the end. Run the following sample code on IDLE:

```
i = 1
while i < 6:
    print(i)
    i += 1
else:
    print("i is no longer less than 6")
```

Ln: 6  Col: 37

## Programming Exercise

In mathematics (yes, Python is used heavily in the world of math), a Fibonacci sequence is one where the next number is the sum of the first two numbers that precedes it.

So, let's say we start with 0, the next number is naturally 1 because nothing preceded 0. Our current sequence is now:

0 1

The next number in the sequence is designated as the sum of the two current numbers. So if we add 0 + 1, then the next number in the Fibonacci sequence is:

0 1 1

That is because 0 + 1 is still 1. The next number in the Fibonacci sequence is 2 since the two numbers that precede it is 1 and 1, which makes two. And now our current sequence is:

0 1 1 2

The next number in our sequence is 3, since the numbers that precede are 1 and 3, which when added together is 3. So our current sequence is now:

$$0\ 1\ 1\ 2\ 3$$

As you might have guessed, the next number in the sequence is 5 because if you take the sum of the two numbers before our current number, it would be 2 + 3. And so on the pattern goes.

Now, your task is to write a program that will ask for user input up to how many Fibonacci digits the user wants to see. And then your program will display the sequence as requested.

To answer this final programming exercise, you will need to use all that you have learned from this book thus far.

The answer will be provided after the key takeaways section of this chapter.

Have fun!

## Key Takeaways
- Loops allow you to reiterate actions within your program

- You need to use the int( ) function to convert the string data from the input( ) function into an integer so you can perform math operations

- The break and continue statements allow you to interrupt the program flow of loops

- The for- and while-loops are the two looping functions in Python

# Answer to Final Programming Exercise

```
Fibonacci Sequence.py - C:/Python Guide/Fibonacci Sequence.py (3.7.4)          —   □   ×
File  Edit  Format  Run  Options  Window  Help
# Program to display the Fibonacci sequence up to n-th term

nterms = int(input("How many terms? "))

# first two terms
n1, n2 = 0, 1
count = 0

# check if the number of terms is valid
if nterms <= 0:
    print("Please enter a positive integer")
elif nterms == 1:
    print("Fibonacci sequence upto",nterms,":")
    print(n1)
else:
    print("Fibonacci sequence:")
    while count < nterms:
        print(n1)
        nth = n1 + n2
        # update values
        n1 = n2
        n2 = nth
        count += 1



                                                                        Ln: 8  Col: 0
```

# Conclusion

Thanks again for taking the time to purchase this book!

You should now have a good understanding of the very basics of Python programming, and programming concepts as well.

Remember that what you have learned so far is only the tip of the iceberg when it comes to the Python programming language and computer programming as a whole.

There are lots of other concepts and features that you will need to learn after going through these principles and exercises.

If you enjoyed this book, please take the time to leave me a review on Amazon. I appreciate your honest feedback, and it really helps me to continue producing high-quality books.

www.ingramcontent.com/pod-product-compliance
Lightning Source LLC
LaVergne TN
LVHW051712050326
832903LV00032B/4151